Mechanic Mike's Machines

Motorcycles

A⁺
Smart Apple Media

Published by Smart Apple Media, an imprint of Black Rabbit Books
P.O. Box 3263, Mankato, Minnesota 56002
www.smartapplemedia.com

Produced by David West Children's Books
6 Princeton Court, 55 Felsham Road, London SW15 1AZ

Designed and illustrated by David West

Copyright © 2016 David West Children's Books

Cataloging-in-Publication Data is available from the Library of Congress.
ISBN 978-1-62588-064-2

Printed in China
CPSIA compliance information: DWCB15CP
311214

9 8 7 6 5 4 3 2 1

Mechanic Mike says:
This little guy will tell you something more about the machine.

Find out what type of engine drives the machine.

Discover something you didn't know.

Is it fast or slow? Top speeds are provided here.

How many crew or people does it carry?

Get your amazing fact here!

Contents

First Motorcycle

The first motorcycles were simply bicycles with small steam engines fitted to them. The first motorcycle with a gasoline **internal combustion engine** was this "Riding Wagon."

Mechanic Mike says:
The Riding Wagon was built by the German inventor Gottlieb Daimler in 1885. It had two stabilizer wheels and was made mainly from wood.

Some people say that the first true motorcycle was invented in 1884 by the Italian inventor Enrico Bernardi, who fitted a gasoline engine to his son's tricycle.

Did you know that three steam-powered motorcycles were invented before the Riding Wagon? They were all pedal bicycles with small steam engines fitted to them.

The Daimler Riding Wagon had room for one person only.

Top speed for this motorcycle was just 7 miles per hour (11 km/h).

The Daimler Riding Wagon had a 264 cc (16 cubic inches), single-cylinder, gasoline internal combustion engine.

Early Motorcycle

Early motorcycles were bicycles with engines fitted to their frames. As the engines became more powerful, the designs, like this Bianchi Freccia Celeste, became more complex.

Early motorcycles had a complex arrangement of struts for front-wheel suspension and no rear suspension.

Did you know that the Bianchi Freccia Celeste was the fastest racer of its day?

It had a top speed of 93 miles per hour (150 km/h).

This motorcycle had room for one rider.

It had a 350 cc (21 cubic inches), single-cylinder, gasoline engine.

Some sidecars were designed so that the motorcycle's rear wheel would also spin the sidecar wheel. This made the vehicle more stable and easier to drive.

Did you know motorcycle sidecar ambulances were used during World War I by the British, French, and American armies? Stretchers were put on special sidecars so that the wounded could be carried to field hospitals more quickly.

The BMW R75 had a top speed of 59 miles per hour (95 km/h).

The BMW R75 could carry three people: one driver and two passengers.

This BMW R75 had a 745 cc (45 cubic inches) flat-twin engine. Flat-twin engines have their cylinders lying horizontally opposite each other.

Sidecar

Until the 1950s sidecars were a popular and cheap alternative to passenger cars. During World War II, troops used sidecar motorcycles like this German BMW R75.

Mechanic Mike says:
Sidecars can be seen in motorsport events from road-racing to motocross.

9

Trial Bike

These specialized motorcycles compete in non-speed events where riders have to complete an obstacle course and avoid touching the ground with their feet. The events are held indoors and outdoors. Trial riders need fine throttle control, good balance, and all-round machine control.

Mechanic Mike says:
Trial events provide exciting viewing as competitors ride up and over incredibly difficult obstacles and balance on thin sections high above the ground.

Trial bikes like this Gas Gas have no seats. The rider performs the entire event standing on the foot rests.

Did you know that when riders complete a section without their feet touching the ground it is called "cleaning the section"?

These bikes are not designed for speed and may have a slow top speed of 40 miles per hour (64 km/h).

Trial bikes are designed for one rider.

This Gas Gas trial bike has a single-cylinder, 125 cc (7.6 cubic inches) engine.

11

Dirt Bike

"Dirt bike" is the term used for an off-road motorcycle. They have long front fork suspension and knobby tires to handle rough terrain. They are used mainly for motocross racing, where competitors race around tough tracks that include steep hills and jumps.

 Dirt bikes have engines ranging in size from 50 cc (3 cubic inches) up to 700 cc (43 cubic inches).

 Dirt bikes are designed for one rider but they can carry a passenger.

 The big 700 cc (43 cubic inches) dirt bikes can travel at more than 110 miles per hour (117 km/h).

 Types of dirt bikes are also used for supermoto where the race circuit includes both road and off-road, and freestyle where riders perform acrobatic stunts.

 Did you know that motocross was originally called scrambling because early races looked like riders were "scrambling" around the circuit?

Mechanic Mike says:
Riding dirt bikes off-road is physically demanding.
Riders often wear special armor under their
clothes to protect themselves if they crash.

13

Sportbike

Sportbikes, like this Fireblade, are designed to look like racing bikes and to be exciting to ride on the road. They have a high performance with good acceleration, cornering, and braking.

Mechanic Mike says:
Sportbikes are made of lightweight materials such as aluminum, titanium, magnesium, and carbon fiber to keep them light. Even the large discs of the disc brakes have holes drilled in them to make them lighter.

In the 1960s British motorcycle enthusiasts raced their sportbikes from café to café. The bikes were known as "café racers."

Did you know that most motorcycles' engines are cooled by air? The Fireblade has its engine cooled by water to stop it from overheating.

This Fireblade goes more than 186 miles per hour (300 km/h).

Although designed for one rider, sportbikes like this one often carry a passenger.

This Fireblade has a 999 cc (61 cubic inches) liquid-cooled, four-cylinder gasoline engine.

Engine sizes of quad bikes range from 19 to 1,000 cc (3 to 61 cubic inches).

Most ATVs are designed to carry one person, but some are designed to carry two people.

ATVs have a typical top speed of around 50 miles per hour (80 km/h).

Did you know that farmers use ATVs with their dogs to round up sheep on large farms? ATVs are powerful enough to pull trailers that can carry sheep, bales of hay, and other farm equipment, which otherwise would need a tractor.

ATVs with six wheels are used by some armies because they are very good over rough terrain and can carry a lot of heavy equipment.

ATV

Motorcycles with four wheels are called ATVs (All-Terrain Vehicles). ATVs are used mainly off-road for fun, racing, and job-related activities such as farming and military. The rider sits on the vehicle and steers with handlebars just like a motorcycle.

Some choppers have three wheels: one in front and two in back.

Choppers are designed to cruise at 60 to 70 miles per hour (97 to 113 km/h).

Choppers like this one are designed to carry one rider.

Did you know that Harley-Davidson motorcycles are affectionately known as "Hogs"?

Choppers come in all shapes and sizes and so do their engines. This one has a 1,450 cc (88 cubic inches), gasoline engine.

Chopper

Motorcycles that have been modified with long body frames and long **telescopic** forks are called "choppers." Some may even be built from scratch with only the engine being supplied by a motorcycle manufacturer.

Mechanic Mike says:
Other types of motorcycles that have been modified are dragster motorcycles. These bikes are designed to go very fast over a quarter-mile-long (0.4-km) strip.

19

Scooter

Scooters are a popular form of two-wheeled transportation. They have smaller wheels and usually smaller engines than motorcycles. This Vespa has bodywork surrounding the rear engine and a foot board for clean travel.

Scooters usually have an engine size from 50 cc up to 200 cc (12 cubic inches).

Scooters like this Vespa can go faster than 85 miles per hour (137 km/h).

Scooters can carry up to two people.

A Vespa 150 was modified by the French military. It incorporated an anti-tank weapon and was designed to be used by paratroopers.

Did you know that Vespa means "wasp" in Italian?

Mechanic Mike says:
Vespas and similar Lambrettas were very popular in the UK during the 1960s when young, fashionable "mods" rode them. Unlike motorcycles of the time, the all-round protection of the scooters' bodywork meant the mods' clothes did not get dirty.

21

Minibike

These little motorcycles are often scaled-down versions of normal-sized motorcycles. Some, like this one, were designed in the 1960s as fun bikes. Minibikes have developed into several different types, such as pocket bikes, pitbikes, and mini choppers.

Small motorcycles called pitbikes look like small dirt bikes. They are used to get quickly around the **pit areas** of racetracks.

Did you know that there are many events for minibike racing, from mini motocross to minimoto for miniature racing bikes called pocket bikes?

This minibike has a top speed of 30 miles per hour (48 km/h).

With a seat height of less than 22 inches (55 cm), there is only room for one person on a minibike!

The first minibikes had 49 cc (3 cubic inches), single-cylinder engines.

Glossary

cc
Cubic centimeters. An engine size is measured by the volume of its combustion chamber.

internal combustion engine
An engine in which the explosion of fuel and air inside cylinders moves pistons up and down, which turns a crankshaft to make a rotating force.

pit area
The area of a racetrack where racing machines have their garages.

telescopic
The ability of a tube to slide into another tube.

Index